Addition Annie

Written by David Gisler • Illustrated by Sarah A. Beise

Children's Press®
A Division of Scholastic Inc.
New York • Toronto • London • Auckland • Sydney
Mexico City • New Delhi • Hong Kong
Danbury, Connecticut

To all my little Debby-Doo friends
— S.A.B.

Reading Consultants

Linda Cornwell
Literacy Specialist

Katharine A. Kane
Education Consultant
(Retired, San Diego County Office of Education
and San Diego State University)

Library of Congress Cataloging-in-Publication Data
Gisler, David.
　　Addition Annie / written by David Gisler; illustrated by Sarah A. Beise.—Rev. ed.
　　　　p. cm. – (Rookie reader)
　　Summary: Addition Annie counts everything around her, from trees and knees to little peas.
　　ISBN 0-516-22560-X (lib. bdg.)　　　　0-516-27378-7 (pbk.)
　　[1. Counting—Fiction. 2. Stories in rhyme.] I. Beise, Sarah A., ill. II. Title. III. Series.
　　PZ8.3.G4246 Ad 2001
　　[E]—dc21　　　　　　　　　　　　　　　　　2001003838

SCHOLASTIC and associated designs are trademarks and/or registered trademarks of Scholastic, Inc. CHILDREN'S PRESS, ROOKIE READER, and A ROOKIE READER and all associated designs are trademarks and/or registered trademarks of Grolier Publishing Company, Inc.
1 2 3 4 5 6 7 8 9 10 R 11 10 09 08 07 06 05 04 03 02

This is Annie.

She adds things up.

1 and 1 are 2.
Annie knows that's true.

2 and 1 are 3.

She counts everything...

trees,

peas,

and many knees.

Addition Annie always adds.

She wants to know
how many.

She counts everything...

buttons,

bows,

and her little fat toes.

Addition Annie
always knows how many.

Word List (30 words)

addition	fat	she
adds	her	that's
always	how	things
and	is	this
Annie	knees	to
are	know	toes
bows	knows	trees
buttons	little	true
counts	many	up
everything	peas	wants

About the Author

When David Gisler wrote this book, he was only in fifth grade, and math was his favorite subject in school. David has been around authors all of his life—including his mother who writes an education column and has written more than fifty books.

About the Illustrator

Sarah A. Beise grew up in North Carolina and now lives in Kansas City, Missouri, with her silly little dog Maggie-Moo.